Dedicated to the grandmothers of the world who hold wisdom in their hearts and to the children of the world who hold the future in their hands. Together, we can all help change how this story ends.

©2020 by Tassia Schreiner
All rights reserved. Published in the United States by Creative Kindness Co.
Visit us on the web at www.creativekindnessco.com
Please email to set up an in person or virtual Author Visit or Creativity Camp for your school or club.
Special thanks to John Schreiner and Angie Griggs. Noah, Anni, and Ezra - I'll love you forever!

"Grandma, I heard a story
of a magical, mythical bee!
Do you know how this tale goes?
Could you share it with me?"

When I was a girl in a flower field, you could still hear them buzzing about."

"Grandma, now wait— you mean that flowers were real too?"

"Thanks to the bees, all kinds of fruit would grow!"

Wherever the bees flew,
there was magic all around!
Sweet treasures just waiting,
springing up from the ground!

You could pick snacks right off of the trees.
Magic and wonder, all thanks to the bees!

Bees pollinated crops,
alfalfa in fields.
This was food for the cows,
abundance of yields.

Big happy cows
meant buckets of milk,
Churned into butter
and ice cream like silk!"

" Wait- pollinate?
Grandma, what does that mean?"

"It's how bees did their magic—
keeping everything green!

"The bees carried life
all over the earth,
But we took for granted
all they were worth."

"Grandma— what happened?
Where did the bees go?"

"My Love, I'm so sorry—
I'm afraid we don't know.

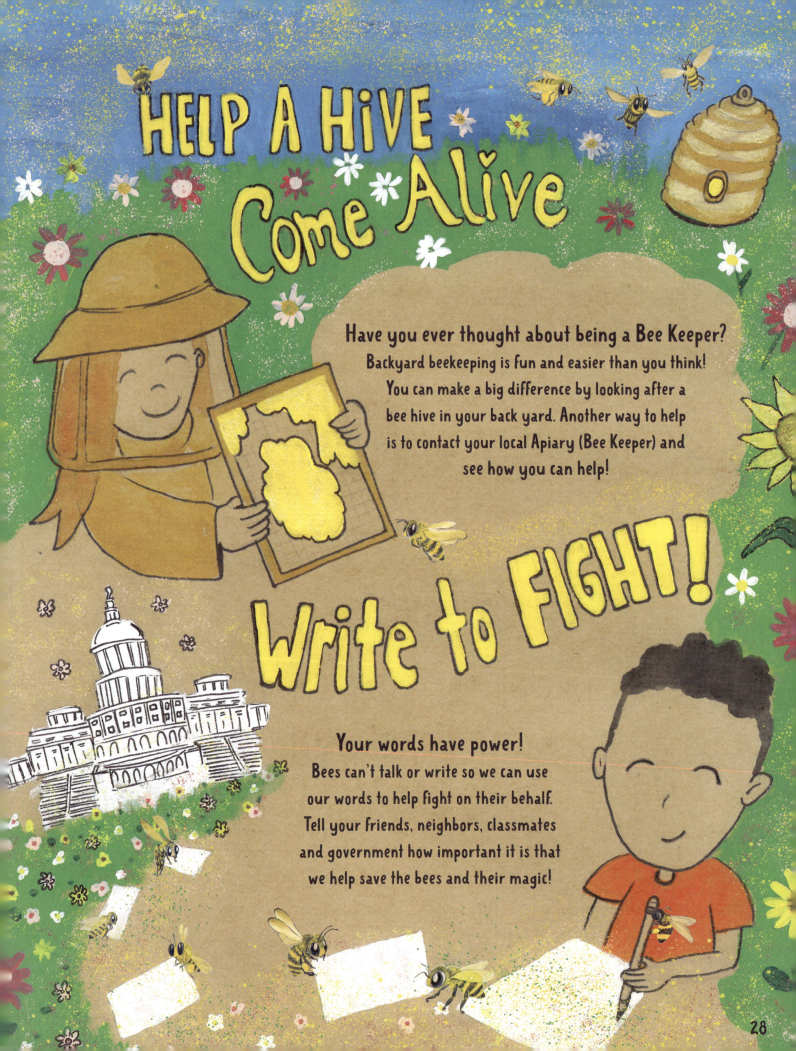

HELP A HIVE Come Alive

Have you ever thought about being a Bee Keeper? Backyard beekeeping is fun and easier than you think! You can make a big difference by looking after a bee hive in your back yard. Another way to help is to contact your local Apiary (Bee Keeper) and see how you can help!

Write to FIGHT!

Your words have power! Bees can't talk or write so we can use our words to help fight on their behalf. Tell your friends, neighbors, classmates and government how important it is that we help save the bees and their magic!

Bees and other pollinators are losing their natural habitats. They need our help! You can create a pollinator garden to help bees find food and refuge. Households and communities can save time and money by dedicating open spaces to growing wildflowers instead of mowing lawns. Planting is easy and growing flowers is a beautiful way to help save the bees!

What if we took a more playful approach to growing our gardens and lawns? Things like clover and dandelion are often looked at as weeds, but they are beautiful and are food for the bees. Organic growing, growing without chemicals that hurt the bees, is a way that we can be kind to the bees and the earth!

WAIT!

IT'S NOT TOO LATE!
You can turn this story around!
Really, if you are reading this first—

STOP AND TURN THE WHOLE BOOK AROUND!
You are in for a treat, this book reads backwards
And for a good reason too!

You and I have the chance to turn this story around in real life and write a better ending with our actions.

Did you know that bees are in danger? We are losing bees in record numbers each year and they need our help!

70% of the food that you enjoy depends on bees to pollinate it. If we lose the bees we could lose all kinds of wonderful things like apples, watermelon, berries, oranges, flowers and even ice cream.

I know that isn't a happy thought... but here is something that is!

You can help! You can make a difference!

Together we can BEE the change!

You may feel little, but the bees are small too—
And they change the world with the magic they do!

With some seeds and some dirt,
and some hope in your heart—
You can be a hero that plants a new start!